CORN

XXX

by Danny Martin

Immerse yourself in the hardships, the successes, the chases, and the raids as you discover the secrets of

MOUNTAIN MOONSHINE.

ISBN 9798387964213

Tom Perry's Laurel Hill Publishing

Thomas D. "Tom" Perry
4443 Ararat Highway
P O Box 11
Ararat VA 24053

276-692-5300
laurelhillpub@gmail.com
https://squareup.com/store/
laurel-hill-publishing-llc

This book was published via an agreement with Tom Perry's Laurel Hill Publishing.

Dedication

This book is dedicated to my beautiful wife, Susan, who I dearly love. I have dragged her through the woods, up mountains, and down mountains to help take photographs and conduct research. Without her help and encouragement, I would never have started this project.

Susan Martin

TABLE OF CONTENTS

CHAPTER 1:
THE BEGINNINGS

In their home countries, the Scotch-Irish were whiskey makers. They were also very strong in their faith. Problems erupted between them and the English government when the government began to interfere with their right to freedom of religion. With the promise of a fresh start and cheap land in the New World, they began to migrate in large numbers to America in 1718, settling along the Appalachian Mountains. Life was tough, and making a living was difficult. Being mostly farmers, they found the land, in many instances, to be unforgiving and the living conditions to be harsh. Imagine an old rickety shack with 6 or 7 kids playing around the house, several hogs in a pen, a cow and a calf grazing around a nearby barn, and chickens running freely in the yard. Imagine a man plowing in a field with a couple of horses or mules and a woman in the house busily canning and drying food from a garden in preparation for a cold winter. This was the life of the Scotch-Irish settler. The settlers often turned to their old ancestral tradition of making whiskey to supplement their incomes. The corn whiskey they made was used like cash to barter for such goods as cloth, gunpowder, sugar, and other items they could not produce themselves. Everything was relatively good for the settlers until 1791, when

Alexander Hamilton proposed an excise tax on whiskey to generate income for the new country that had just won independence from Great Britain. The excise tax was adopted, and problems immediately began. The amount of the tax was about equal to the profit which was being made from the whiskey. If paid, the taxes would represent a great hardship to the farmer trying to make a living and support his family. Unable to afford the license fees and taxes, the whiskey makers refused to comply, launching a battle with the Federal government that has lasted until today. Even the procedure to pay the taxes created an additional burden on the whiskey makers. The new law required the tax to be paid, in person and in cash, to the Federal Revenue Officer assigned to the county. This often meant a lengthy trip over rough dirt roads since the Revenue Officer severed multiple counties. In 1794, farmers in western Pennsylvania became violent and rebelled in protest against the excise tax. However, George Washington quickly quelled the uprising, known as the Whiskey Rebellion, by sending 13,000 militia members to the area. As time passed, a new agency, the Internal Revenue Service, was created to handle the collection of all Federal taxes, including the taxes on whiskey. A special group of officers within the IRS was assigned to ferret out illegal whiskey operations, destroy the stills, and arrest the operators. These officers became known as "revenuers," reflecting the name of their agency. But nothing stopped the determined whiskey makers. The threat of being arrested and jailed, the possibility of having their equipment destroyed, or even the chance of being shot in a raid were all viewed as a risk worth taking. The whiskey makers employed many tricks to stay ahead of the revenuers. They located their operations deep in the forest under heavy leaf cover to hide their illegal stills. Because a fire was required in their whiskey making process (to be discussed later), they made their illegal whiskey at night by the light of the moon. Thus, their whiskey became known as "moonshine" and the whiskey makers as "moonshiners." (They were also frequently called "bootleggers" because some carried a flask with illegal liquor hidden in their boot tops.) Many moonshiners believed that by locating their stills under the leaf cover the smoke would be absorbed. They referred to this as "smoke swallowing." This belief was not entirely correct, but the leaf cover did help to both hold the smoke close to the ground and to break up the rising smoke. A wisp of smoke rising from a remote wooded hollow has led to the downfall of many moonshiners!!!! Modern moonshiners avoid the "smoke problem" by using propane in their distilling process.

Today, stills may appear in old buses, trailers, caves, basements, buildings, barns, and even on kitchen stoves. It's important to remember that although the old moonshiners were mostly uneducated and many had never been to school a day in their life, most were very intelligent and devised numerous innovations to increase their production. However, as you will see, some of their innovations to improve their production output were not always beneficial to the consumer. As discussed previously, the early settlers used their whiskey to trade or barter for various goods. The concept of bartering appeared again in the Virginia mountains in the 1900s.

From 1920 to 1933, Prohibition was implemented by the Federal government. Prohibition banned the manufacture, importation, sale, and transport of alcoholic beverages. In the meantime, the Great Depression (1929-1939) was taking its toll on the mountain people. Many mountain people were finally beginning to recover from the impacts of the Civil War. During the war, most Southerners converted any cash assets to money the Confederate States of America issued. After the war, the Confederate money was worthless. The mountain farmers had very little but they did know how to make moonshine. And the timing was perfect. With Prohibition in effect, the demand for whiskey was extremely high, and the moonshiners were ready to furnish the supply. Many moonshiners survived and thrived during the Great Depression by using their illegal whiskey to, once again, barter for the goods and services they needed for survival.

Life was difficult for the early Scotch-Irish settlers. Large families, poor living conditions, and hard work was their routine.

Early settlers relied on their homemade whiskey to barter for needed items they could not produce.

To avoid detection, illegal whiskey makers made their brew at night by the light of the moon, hence the term "moonshine."

A small wisp of smoke rising from a remote hollow was a dead giveaway that an illicit moonshine still was operating. Modern moonshiners use propane to solve that problem!!!!

Moonshiners operate in many places to avoid being detected, even on kitchen stoves. Even small stills, like the one pictured, require a license to be legal.

Some superstitious moonshiners carried good luck charms, believing the charms would keep them free from the revenuers. Note the "lucky horseshoe" hanging on the cap arm.

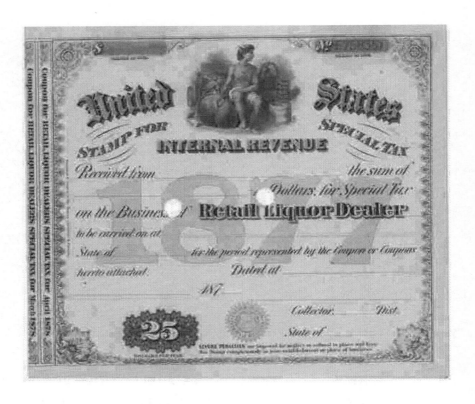

To be legal, whiskey makers were required to pay taxes on their liquor. A special stamp was issued and affixed to the whiskey container to show that taxes had been paid. The whiskey was then referred to as "stamped" whiskey. The above photo is a whiskey stamp from 1877.

CHAPTER 2:
WHAT'S IN THAT POWERFUL STUFF?

When getting started, the moonshiner had two tasks to consider, the moonshine ingredients and the still equipment. We will first examine the ingredients necessary to manufacture the moonshine. The mixture required to create the alcohol is called "mash," and the actual act of mixing up the ingredients is called "mashing-in." Barrels, referred to as "mash barrels," were used to mash-in. More modern moonshiners used boxes constructed from plywood, fifty-five gallon steel drums, or blue plastic chemical drums to mash-in. The mash ingredients include ground corn, malt, yeast, and water. Some moonshiners grew their corn, while others bought it from other farmers. Corn would be allowed to stand in the field until it hardened. After harvesting, the corn would be ground in one of the many water wheel mills. In later days, the moonshiner could purchase corn meal already ground and bagged from local stores. Several reactions occur in the mash as it produces alcohol. Corn contains starches with long molecular chains of glucose (sugar). The malt has enzymes which break down the long sugar chains, enabling the yeast to convert the sugar to alcohol as the mash is allowed to ferment. The malt used to make moonshine was usually made from corn or barley. It was soaked in water and allowed to sprout. After drying, the sprouted grain would be ground into a powder before being used in the mashing-in process. The mash must be occasionally stirred to break up the crusty cap which would form on the surface. This was done with a "mash rake." The mash rake was made from a forked stick with wire stretched across the forks or from a stick with a crook at one end. Holes would be drilled on one side of the crook, and pegs inserted to form a comb-like device. As the mash ferments, the alcohol content increases, reaching a maximum at some point. The moonshiners knew when the maximum amount of alcohol had developed in the mash when "dog heads" or large bubbles began to boil up in the mash. The mash had to be processed as soon as possible because the alcohol would start to evaporate. Fermented mash was also known as "still beer." Often, the entire family was involved in the moonshining operation. Can't you just imagine some small child, who had been sent to check on the condition of the mash, running back to the field where his daddy was plowing while shouting, "Daddy, daddy, we got dog heads!" Priorities had a way of quickly changing at this magic moment! If everything is done exactly right and the mash has reached its maximum alcoholic content, 100 gallons of mash will yield about 10 gallons of moonshine. If revenuers discovered a still operation, they would also periodically check the mash to get an idea of when the mash would be ready to process. They would use this information to plan a raid, knowing the operator would most likely be at the still site and provide them the opportunity to make an arrest. The time it took for the mash to ferment largely depended on the temperature. The mash took much longer to ferment during colder weather. But the innovative moonshiner devised ways to help overcome this problem. The moonshiner had learned from shoveling out his barn stalls that the manure always seemed hot. Of course, the heat was produced by the bacterial action going on within the manure. The moonshiner made use of his discovery by packing manure around his mash barrels or mash boxes to provide insulation and generate heat to speed up the fermentation process. By accident, if a bit of manure happened to slip into the mash, NO PROBLEM, just a little extra flavor!!!!! Unfortunately, for the moonshine consumer, some unscrupulous moonshiners placed old car batteries in the mash boxes or barrels, believing the battery acids would speed up the fermentation process. Some others put lye in the mash to speed things up. Unlike the old Scotch-Irish settlers who took great pride in the quality of their whiskey, moonshining, in some cases, became an activity driven by greed. A well known moonshiner in Franklin County, Virginia, once stated, "I make moonshine to sell, not to drink." As sugar became easy to obtain, moonshiners found they could eliminate the malt and use sugar as one of the critical components when mashing-in. The corn still flavored the brew while the yeast converted the sugar to alcohol. It was common practice to cover the mash barrels and mash boxes to keep all the critters out. I once found a small still that had thirteen barrels of fermenting mash. The mash could not be "run" (processed) simultaneously in this situation. The moonshiner would have mashed-in over several days so the barrels of mash would reach its maximum alcohol content at varying times. This way, the moonshiner could continuously run for days, with mash reaching its maximum alcoholic content. The thirteen barrels were covered with roll roofing material. I lifted the cover to look at the mash. In addition to a layer of insects, I was met with two beady eyes looking back at me. It was a dead 'possum that had gotten in the barrel and probably had too much to drink. I guess he passed out and drowned. Do I think the moonshiner would have destroyed the mash? NO WAY. Just a bit of an extra kick!!!! I raided the still two days later. When the mash has fermented and is ready to run, the moonshiner's next task is to remove the alcohol from the mash mixture. This is done by distilling the mash in equipment specially designed for making moonshine. Occasionally, some moonshiners made brandy in their stills, particularly around Christmas. The process of making brandy was the same as making corn whiskey, except fruit was used instead of corn. The mash for brandy was referred to as "pummies." The fruit pummies, usually made from apples or peaches, was allowed to ferment and then distilled just as with corn whiskey. Peach or apple brandy commanded much higher prices than regular moonshine. It has been said that around Christmas, many years ago, some moonshiners would make an annual trip to town to visit the judges, sheriff, and Commonwealth's Attorney to sneak them a present of a quart of their highly prized, and ILLEGAL, brandy.

It all starts here – THE CORNFIELD.

One of the many water wheel mills located along the
Virginia mountains' streams.

Wooden barrels or boxes were often used to "mash- in" (mix the ingredients). Later moonshiners used steel drums. Today, blue plastic chemical drums are popular for use as "mash barrels."

Making moonshine was often a family affair. The knowledge acquired to make moonshine was handed down from generation to generation and continues even today.

A mash rake was used to break up the crusty cap,
which would form on the top of the fermenting mash.

A moonshiner uses a mash rake to stir his mash.

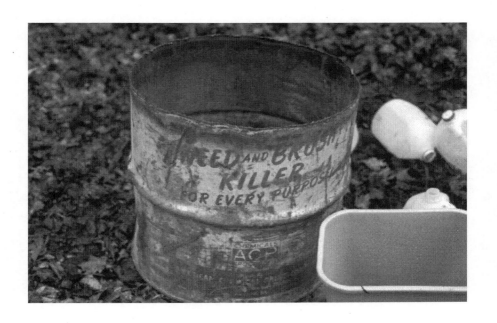

This barrel was used to mash-in. Take a look at what originally came in it!!!

CHAPTER 3:
THE EQUIPMENT AND THE PROCESS

The moonshining equipment has several components. The first piece of equipment we will discuss is the vessel that contains the mash. It is usually referred to as the "still." It may also be called the "kettle" or the "pot." All the components collectively may also be referred to as the still. Old day moonshine still parts were made from copper. As the tradition evolved, other materials were used. We will discuss those also. The still kettle was placed on a horseshoe shaped arrangement of rocks called the "furnace." Later moonshiners used concrete blocks to build their furnace. The fermented mash would be poured into the still, and the removable "cap" would be installed. A wire or chain, called the "bale" would be fastened across the top of the cap to keep it from blowing off during the cooking process. The joint where the cap seats on the still kettle would be sealed with a paste made from mud (particularly red clay if available) or by a paste made from flour and water. Wood would be put in the furnace and set on fire. Modern moonshiners use propane for "cooking" their mash. The old moonshiners knew that alcohol boiled at a lower temperature than water. Alcohol boils at 173 degrees Fahrenheit, and water at 212 degrees Fahrenheit. The moonshiner's goal was to keep the mash temperature between those limits so only the alcohol would boil and produce alcohol steam. Although the early moonshiner lacked thermometers or any other instrumentation, he knew the right amount of wood to put on the fire to maintain the right temperature. The steam produced would collect at the cap's top and flow through the "cap arm" to the next still component. If the moonshiner miscalculated the amount of wood and the mash got too hot and boiled over or "puked," as the moonshiner called it, the cap arm could plug up. This was a hazardous condition, and the still could blow up and cover the moonshiner(s) with scalding mash! The next component of the still operation is called the "thumper" or "doubler." The thumper can be made from a wooden barrel or fabricated from metal. It has a 25% - 40% capacity of the still kettle. Picture a barrel with a pipe, the "long thump rod," entering the top of the barrel and extending to a few inches off the bottom of the barrel. Imagine another pipe, the "short thump rod," extending through the top of the barrel just a few inches below the top surface of the barrel. This is how the thumper is constructed. The thumper would be partially filled with fresh, fermented mash or moonshine with a low alcoholic content. The hot steam flowing through the cap arm enters the thumper through the long thump rod. The steam eventually causes the alcohol in the thumper to boil and generate its own steam. As the pressure forces the flow through the long thump rod, bubbles form as the flow exits the long thump rod. The bubbles create a loud thumping noise, hence the name thumper. All the alcohol steam now gathers in the top of the thumper and is forced through the short thump rod to the next component of the still. The thumper effectively doubles the alcoholic content of the steam headed to the next component of the still. Alcohol steam is produced in the still kettle and in the thumper. Many of the old moonshiners didn't have a thumper. The resulting moonshine had a low alcoholic content or low "proof." The proof number is twice the percentage of alcohol in the whiskey. For example, moonshine containing 50 percent alcohol is 100 proof. The moonshiner, who didn't use a thumper, would drain and clean the still kettle after the first run. Then, he would pour the low proof moonshine in the kettle and run (distill) it again to increase the proof. This procedure would generally be repeated a third time to achieve the desired proof. You may have seen some cartoons, pictures, or TV programs with a jug of moonshine with three Xs painted on the jug. The three Xs indicate the number of times the moonshine was distilled. Now, only one stage remains in the process. After the steam leaves the thumper, it flows into the "worm." The worm is a coiled piece of tubing. The tubing is totally submerged in a barrel or wooden box called a "flake stand." Cold water continuously flows into the top of the flake stand and out of the bottom. The cold water surrounding the worm causes the hot alcohol steam inside the worm to condense to liquid moonshine. Making the worm sometimes presented a problem. You may have been washing your car or watering your flowers with a hose when the water flow suddenly turns into a dribble. A short investigation usually reveals the hose has become crimped. The same thing can happen when tubing is bent in a tight radius, like that of the worm. If a valuable piece of tubing crimps while trying to form the coiled shape of the worm, it is almost impossible to remove the crimped area. The moonshiner lacked any specialized tube bending equipment, but being very innovative, he was able to solve the problem. The first step was to find a tree of the correct diameter and cut it down, leaving a stump about chest high. Next, the moonshiner would fill his tubing with tightly packed sand. One end of the tubing would then be attached to the bottom of the stump and carefully bent around the stump to form the worm. Now all the moonshiner had to do was to slide the worm over the stump and clean out the sand. Pretty smart!!!! After cars became popular, another innovation began to appear at some stills. Instead of going to all the trouble to make a worm, the moonshiners discovered that the worm could be replaced with an old car radiator. It was effortless and cheap to do, and it worked well. The moonshiner placed the radiator in the flake stand where the worm usually was. The short thump rod would be connected to the top of the radiator. As the steam flowed from the thumper, it entered the radiator and traveled through all the radiator's intricate passages. The steam inside the radiator condenses when submerged in cold water, and liquid moonshine comes out the bottom. One radiator may not be enough to fully condense the steam on a huge still. In such a situation, radiators could be connected in series, and the entire bank of radiators submerged in a flake stand. Although the radiators worked quite well to condense the alcohol steam, significant problems for the consumer could result. Car radiators were put together with lead solder. While traveling through the radiator ports, lead could be picked up by the steam and transferred to the resulting moonshine. Many cases of lead poisoning resulted from the use of car radiators and from other sources, which we will also talk about.

Lead poisoning can cause extreme illness, blindness, and even death.

The still kettle was placed on a furnace constructed from rocks or cement blocks.

The bale is a wire or chain that keeps the cap from blowing off during the cooking stage.

The number of Xs indicates how many times the
moonshine was distilled.

The thumper (in the middle) doubles the alcoholic content of the steam before it is condensed. The thumper was also frequently referred to as the "doubler."

The worm was difficult to fabricate and was prized by the moonshiner.

THE DISTILLATION PROCESS

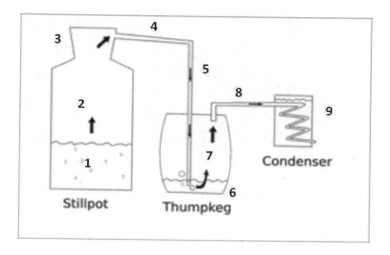

Boiling mash (1) produces alcohol steam (2). The steam gathers in the cap (3) and is forced through the cap arm (4). Steam flows through the long thump rod (5) and causes the low proof alcohol or fresh mash (6) to boil. The alcohol enriched steam (7) flows through the short thump rod (8) into the worm (9) where it condenses to liquid moonshine.

Moonshiners concerned with only making money could market a product that could contain poisonous methyl alcohol, lead, antifreeze, lye, or even battery acid residue.

Stills come in different shapes and sizes and are made from various materials. This small copper kettle was operating on a remote, crystal clear stream not far from the Patrick / Henry County, Virginia, county line. It probably produces between 1 and 2 quarts of illegal moonshine per run. IS THIS REALLY WORTH TAKING A CHANCE ON A FELONY CONVICTION?

This large copper kettle still probably dates to the late 1700s. Note the craftsmanship. You won't find one of these in the woods today!!!

CHAPTER 4:
THE SUBMARINE

Another innovation began to appear in the moonshining culture. This was the "submarine still." The submarine still looks like an army tank without the tracks. The submarine still has the same components as the kettle still: the cap, thumper, and the worm. It offers several advantages to the moonshiner, which can increase his production. First, it is very easy to build. A wooden frame is built, and sheet metal is nailed over the frame. Poplar wood was the wood of choice used to make the frame. It is soft and easy to work. It doesn't contain tannic acid like the oak. It doesn't have resins like pine. And poplar is relatively light.

Copper sheet metal was sometimes used, but galvanized tin was cheaper and usually used by most moonshiners. After the submarine still had been finished, it would usually be submerged in water to allow the wood to swell and seal any leak which might be present. Another advantage was size. The submarine stills could be huge, in some cases over 1000 gallons. The submarine still offered a third and important advantage: the moonshiner could mash-in directly in the still, avoiding all the barrels. A small fire could be built under the submarine to preheat the mash and speed up the fermentation process. The submarine still also made it easy for mass production operations. In an operation like the one pictured at the end of the chapter, the moonshiners would mash- in at the first still, let's say today. They may mash-in the second still tomorrow, the next still the next day, and so on until they get to the last one. By then, the first still's mash had fermented and would be ready to run. The moonshiner would place the cap on, move a thumper and worm in place, build a fire in the furnace, and run the mash off. When finished, he might pour in sugar and yeast to allow the mash to ferment again. He would then move to the next still and repeat the process, then to the third, and so on. By the time he reached the end, the first one would be ready to run again. Some moonshiners who didn't particularly care about the quality of their product may have used the same mash over and over, maybe even seven or eight times. The mash may rot and turn black. It has been reported that sometimes the mash would be so rancid and give off such a stench that buzzards could be seen in the trees around the still. Whiskey resulting from such practices was appropriately referred to as black pot, rotgut, bust-head, or pop-skull!!!! The term "black pot" referred to the blackened color of the still equipment due to leaks and spills of the rotten mash. When the rotten mash was finally discarded, it was often used to feed hogs. There's nothing like 100 proof bacon! Despite the advantages the submarine offered, it also could have a serious drawback.

The moonshiner learned that he could make very large, high capacity stills. One sheet of tin would not be wide enough to cover the large wooden frame. So, he had to use two sheets, resulting in a seam that had to be sealed. The seams were sealed with lead solder. As with the use of radiators, lead could easily contaminate the moonshine. Large submarine stills could have over fifteen hundred linear inches of solder. Whiskey from large submarine stills using radiators to condense the steam could potentially contain lethal amounts of lead. This lack of care and the greed of some moonshiners added more "fuel to the fire" in the ongoing battle with the revenuers.

The first step in building a submarine still is to build a wooden frame. This one is shown upside down.

You know it's got to be good mash when it attracts buzzards!!!!!

Submarine stills are easily adapted to large, mass production operations like this one. This operation was one of the largest ever destroyed. It was raided in Franklin County, Virginia, in 1922.

The submarine still was easy to make and offered several advantages to the moonshiner.

CHAPTER 5:
MOONSHINE: THE FINISHED PRODUCT

After a run is complete, there's still a lot of work to do. As the still run progresses, the proof of the moonshine diminishes, and it must be blended or "proofed." The first condensed liquid from the worm is called the "foreshots." It is poisonous, containing methyl alcohol and other toxic substances, and must be discarded. The foreshots will be roughly four fluid ounces for every five gallons of still capacity. A one hundred gallon still would produce about eighty fluid ounces or roughly five pints of foreshots. The remainder of the run can be divided into three, roughly equal, parts: the heads, the hearts, and the tailings. The heads are over 160 proof and considered undrinkable unless you want to knock your hat off!!! Heads are saved for proofing. The hearts range from around 130 proof to 160 proof. Many drinkers prefer whiskey in this range. The tailings range from the lowest detectable alcohol to 130 proof. Many moonshiners wanted to blend their whiskey to around 100 proof. In the early days, it was a lot of guesswork. Modern moonshiners can use a hydrometer to be more exact. Moonshiners used water or low proof alcohol to mix with alcohol of higher proof to achieve just the right blend. Some greedy moonshiners resorted to using rubbing (methyl) alcohol or antifreeze to proof their moonshine. Guess they didn't want their customers to freeze up in the winter!!!!! The early moonshiners used three methods to proof their alcohol. In the "flame-up" test, the moonshiner would carefully blend a small amount of alcohol and throw it in on a fire. If it flamed up and burned, it was still above 100 proof. The gunpowder method was similar to the flame-up test. Moonshine would be mixed with a small amount of gunpowder. A flame would be applied to the mixture. If the moonshine caught on fire and ignited the gunpowder, it was considered above 100 proof. The third method of proofing is called "reading the bead." If a container of moonshine is shaken, small bubbles or "beads" form on the surface of the liquid. The moonshiner would place some of his blend in a small vial and shake it to create a bead. If the bead floated about half above the surface and half below, the alcohol was approximately 100 proof.

Any leftover tailings or other low proof moonshine could be redistilled or used in the thumper. After the proofing task was completed, the moonshine was put in containers. Early moonshiners preferred half-gallon fruit jars, while modern day moonshiners mostly use one gallon plastic jugs. Moonshine is known by various names, including corn squeezins, tiger's breath, white lightning, mountain dew, panther sweat, kickapoo joy juice, clear, and others. The origin of the name White Lightning has an interesting history. Some of the old timers believed there were two kinds of lightning, red lightning, and white lightning. They thought a fire started by red lightning could be quickly extinguished, while a fire started by white lightning could not be put out by any means.

Following a big gulp of high proof moonshine, they believed that a fire had started in their insides that could never be extinguished, thus WHITE LIGHTNING!!!! After the proofing and bottling, the moonshiner had to get his whiskey from the still location. In the early days, this usually meant hauling it out on his back or packing it out on a mule, where applicable. The moonshiner had to be careful about leaving any sign of his presence. Revenuers were always vigilantly looking for tracks, paths, and other signs of human traffic in areas where it didn't belong. The old moonshiners often took their whiskey to some hidden location near their homes. Sometimes, it would be sold from the home to trusted customers. At other times, the moonshiner might deliver his product. Either way always involved the risk of being caught. As time passed and stills became larger, the moonshiner found new, more distant markets. Often, truckloads of moonshine left the mountains, destined for large northern cities such as New York, Cincinnati, Chicago, and Detroit, where it would be sold under the counter at local "nip joints." These establishments were known as "blind tigers." One such blind tiger was located near Fairy Stone State Park in Patrick County, Virginia, on Route 57. It was known as the Tin Shack because the building was covered with tin. It had a local reputation, being known for its gambling and availability of moonshine. Fearful of being caught, the operators kept their moonshine across the road, hidden under a stump. Hiding places varied. Behind the Fairy Stone Lake Dam, a moonshiner (and farmer on the side) had a cornfield. There was a large stump in the middle of the cornfield. Under the stump was a large cavity where he cached his whiskey. When someone came to his home to buy his moonshine, they were asked to wait while he went to the nearby field to get the whiskey. Another man who sold the illicit whiskey had a large hole dug in the side of an embankment where Route 57 in Henry County, Virginia, passed over. The hole was covered with plywood and camouflaged with leaves. Hundreds of cars passed over the stashed moonshine every day. Moonshine has inspired books to be written, stories to be told, movies to be made, and songs to be sung. Below is a short list of songs where you can learn more about the moonshine culture. Just Google the title, followed by the word "song." Click on it, step back in history, and enjoy.

Daddy's Moonshine Still
The Ballad of Thunder Road
Good Old Mountain Dew
Franklin County Moonshine
White Lightning
Copperhead Road
Bootlegger's Boy
Tear My Stillhouse Down
Good Corn Liquor
The Moonshine Song
Shine

Whether a neighbor, a passerby, a northern city dweller, or a local judge, there has always been a market for moonshine, and there probably always will be!

The first condensate from the worm, the foreshots, is very toxic and should not be consumed.

When shaken, the position of the bubble or "bead" on the surface of the moonshine is indicative of the proof. If the bead floated about half above the surface and half below, it was approximately 100 proof.

Moonshine was known by different names. Most described its potency or appearance, such as panther's breath or clear.

Some moonshiners would hide 'shine in a hollow stump for their regular, trusted customers. The customer would retrieve the jar and leave money in the stump. Anyone "forgetting" to leave the money just might find themselves in DEEP TROUBLE.

This massive hole was dug underneath Route 57 near the Patrick / Henry County line. It was filled with cases of half gallon jars containing moonshine. Hundreds of cars passed overhead each day.

The "Tin Shack" was a "nip joint" or "blind tiger" located on Route 57 near Fairy Stone State Park in Patrick County, Virginia.

Half gallon jars of moonshine were hidden in an old stump across Route 57 from the old "Tin Shack," a "blind tiger" in Patrick County, Virginia.

Looks like a happy customer. Bet that 'shine has been aged. Must be at least TWO WEEKS OLD!!!!!

CHAPTER 6:
TRUE MOONSHINE STORIES

The following is a series of true stories involving Southwest Virginia moonshiners, particularly Patrick, Franklin, and Floyd Counties. In some of the stories, the names have been changed or omitted to "protect the not so innocent!" Some of the stories are funny, some sad. They all help define the moonshine heritage and culture in the Appalachian Mountains.

Buck Got the Last Laugh

An old mining boom town, Fayerdale, once stood where the lake is located at Fairy Stone State Park in Patrick County, Virginia. In its heyday, around 1910, the town hosted approximately 2,500 people and numerous businesses. Since no cars existed, travel by horseback and wagon was the standard mode of transportation to and from the remotely located town. Because of the volume of horse travel and the need to frequently repair busted mining equipment, the local blacksmith shop was critical to the town's survival. One of the local blacksmiths was a moonshiner who grew his own corn.

In the Fall, when the corn had hardened in the field, the moonshiner knew it was time to harvest the corn and take it to the mill to be ground into meal for the major component of his mash. So, off he went to his corn field on a wagon pulled by a stubborn old mule named Buck. Everything went smoothly as the moonshiner preceded up and down the rows of corn while pulling the ears of corn from the stalks and tossing them into the wagon. Eventually, the wagon was full, and the moonshiner was ready to return home. But Buck had different plans. He sat down and refused to move. Now if you've never seen a mule sit down, it's just like a dog. He sits back on his butt and keeps his front legs straight. I'm sure Buck got cussed at and maybe worse, but he refused to move. Finally, the frustrated moonshiner had an idea.

He probably had heard the old saying, "You have to build a fire under

some people to get them to move."
With that in mind and the fact that the
corn was dry, the moonshiner went to
the wagon and pulled the shucks from
several ears of corn. He stuffed the
shucks under Buck's rear end and set
them on fire. Now Buck wasn't
burned, but he did decide it was time
to move. Buck, much to the
moonshiners satisfaction, stood up
and began to move. However, he only
moved eight feet or so and sat down
again. But during his short movement,
he pulled the wagon over the fire. The
wagon caught on fire and burned all
the corn. BUCK GOT THE LAST LAUGH.

The Philpott Train Station

A train station operated by Norfolk and Western (now Norfolk and Southern) was once located in the small community of Philpott in Henry County, Virginia. Like many other small stations, the Philpott train station has long been gone. A small legal distillery was operating not too far from the train station. However, with the coming of the Prohibition movement, the distillery was closed, and all of the whiskey was impounded, destined to be destroyed. I come from a sawmill family. My daddy owned a mill that he operated for many years.

Occasionally, something at the mill would break. The replacement parts would often be large and usually heavy, prohibiting US mail shipment. Since back in the early days when carriers such as UPS and Federal Express did not exist, my dad had to rely on the rails for deliveries of items to get the mill going again. On one such occasion, when he was notified that a needed part was at the train station, I went with him to pick it up. This would have been around 1952. This was the first time I had ever been to a train station, so I wanted to check everything out and immediately disappeared in a back room of the station. I saw a lot of crates, some pieces of farm equipment, and something else that caught my eye. My exploration was cut short when I heard my daddy holler for me. On the way home, he asked me where I had gone. I remember telling him that I went "out back."

Little train stations similar to the one above served most all communities along the tracks of Norfolk and Western (now Norfolk and Southern).

Then I asked about the item that caught my eye. "Daddy, why are all those holes in the floor?" I had seen dozens of holes about an inch in diameter all over the floor. Daddy explained Prohibition and told me that the whiskey impounded from the legal distillery had been stored at the train station until it could be shipped out and later destroyed. But the locals had learned that the whiskey had been stored at the train station and had slipped underneath the station one night and, with augers, drilled holes in the floor. The augers also drilled holes in the barrels, which were drained into the innovative locals' containers. The holes in the floor were never patched and remained until the station was abandoned and torn down. Can you imagine the look on the authorities' faces when they arrived to load the barrels only to find they were all EMPTY!!!

The Fayerdale Train

We talked about the old mining town, Fayerdale, and the train station at Philpott. The Norfolk and Western train ran the route on a spur line along Goblintown Creek (named for the large wild turkey population) and the Smith River. The train carried iron ore, passengers, fruits from the local orchard, barrels of American Chestnuts, tannin bark, sacks of mail from the Post Office, and lumber. It also carried stamped (taxed) whiskey from the local, legal DeHart distillery warehouse at Fayerdale. The trip from Fayerdale was usually uneventful, but the return trip was sometimes very stressful for the engineers. On return to Fayerdale, the train would transport passengers, goods for the general store, and mail. But often, moonshiners would walk onto the tracks, armed with a rifle or shotgun, and stop the train. They would force the engineers to load their illegal, untaxed moonshine on the train and deliver it to Fayerdale for use by the residents. The untaxed whiskey was much cheaper and highly sought after. It was said that if the engineers didn't comply, they wouldn't be engineers much longer. This probably meant that

they would not be fired, but FIRED AT!!!

This old Norfolk and Western locomotive traveled from Fayerdale to the community of Philpott. Over the twelve mile trip, the train hauled many commodities made in and around Fayerdale, including legal, "stamped" whiskey. On the return trips to Fayerdale, the train would often be stopped, and the engineers were forced to haul ILLEGAL MOONSHINE back to Fayerdale for consumption by the locals.

Heck With This, We're Going Home

Moonshining was hard work. Imagine carrying heavy still equipment and hundreds of pounds of ground corn, sugar, jars, and yeast, on your back, into the woods. Now imagine carrying out hundreds of gallons of moonshine. Some moonshiners used mules, where practical, to transport their materials to the still and bring their moonshine from the still site. Mules left tracks and left other sign. Revenuers were constantly watching for anything that might suggest an illegal whiskey making operation was going on. This often meant checking old logging roads and other access points, which could lead to a good moonshining site. Once, an enterprising moonshiner wanted to set up a new still. He had chosen a location where some logging operations had recently occurred. The moonshiner figured that, with all the recent activity, a few mule tracks wouldn't be noticed. So, he approached his brother-in-law, who was also well known in the moonshine community, about borrowing his two mules to take his still equipment in. The mules were obtained, and the still equipment was taken into the perfect location deep in the woods along a crystal clear stream. But, the moonshiner left too much evidence of his illicit plan or told the wrong person, or someone saw him.

Revenuers raided the still and destroyed it before it was even set up. When the revenuers found the still, guess what else they found?

TWO MULES TIED TO A TREE. Revenuers are also innovative. They knew that mules have a powerful homing instinct. They released the mules, which immediately headed home, with the revenuers closely following behind. When they reached the owner's home, the revenuers went to work. They accused the mule's owner of having the still. He denied any knowledge of the still. He kept a level head and told the revenuers that his mules had been stolen. He affirmed his religious faith to the revenuers and said he would pray for his poor mules who were forced to participate in such a sinful endeavor as moonshining.   After seeing they were getting nowhere, the revenuers gave up, and THE MULES WERE HAPPY TO BE HOME.

Some moonshiners used mules to pack in their still supplies, sometimes including hundreds of pounds of sugar, corn meal, and other incidental items. The moonshiner had to be careful and cover his tracks to avoid detection.

No Business Mountain

It seems that on a sunny afternoon many years ago, a gentleman, Mr. Woods, was sitting on the front porch of his residence located near the foot of a large, un-named mountain. He saw a city feller walking by, headed towards the mountain, but he didn't say anything. A while later, Mr. Woods heard gunshots coming from the mountain. Soon, the city feller came running from the direction of the mountain. Mr. Woods spoke out, "Where you been?" The city feller responded, "I've been up on that mountain where I had no business." The stranger had unknowingly walked into the middle of a moonshining operation and was mistaken for a revenuer. Soon the story got around, and the name "NO BUSINESS MOUNTAIN" stuck forever and is now one of the most prominent landmarks in Patrick County, Virginia.

The Moonshine Murders

Mountain folks have always been known for holding grudges, as evidenced by numerous famous family feuds. This next story is a good example. The story begins in the summer of 1927 on a small creek in what is now Fairy Stone State Park. A man named Jack Hall was operating a moonshine still on the creek. One day, a teenage boy, we'll call him EN, came to the still and wanted to buy a pint of whiskey. Now moonshiners were performing illegal activities, and many would shoot you in a heartbeat, but they had principles. Jack knew the boy was underage and refused to sell the moonshine to him. EN told Jack he knew some important information about his still that he needed to know but would not tell Jack unless he sold him the whiskey. Finally, Jack gave in and sold the whiskey. EN told Jack that David Cox, another moonshiner, had reported his still to the revenuers. This information infuriated Jack Hall because one of the greatest transgressions you could do was to report somebody's still!!! And, in fact, several days later, the revenuers raided and destroyed the still and arrested Jack. Jack was released on bond and promised to retaliate, although David Cox denied having any part in reporting Hall's still. The revenuers also stated that David Cox had not reported the still. But Jack would not listen and had made up his mind. He knew where David Cox's still was located and went there and destroyed it. Hall had also borrowed a still from Tom Shelton to get back in business following his raid. When Hall destroyed David Cox's still, Cox vowed to get even. He had learned where Hall had set up the borrowed still. He went there, took the still to the road in front of Hall's house, and chopped it up with an axe. Hall was extremely angry, but he had another plan in lieu of violence. Jack Hall went to the Sheriff's Office in Stuart, Virginia, to swear out a warrant for David Cox for, of all things, manufacturing illegal whiskey. The warrant was issued, but Hall went one step further. He asked the Sheriff if he could keep the warrant and make the arrest himself. Now, remember, Jack was not a law enforcement officer, had no authority of any kind, and was out on bond for Federal felony charges. Despite all this, the Patrick County Sheriff told Hall to keep the warrant and make the arrest. Rumor was that the Sheriff didn't want to get involved because he was accepting payoffs from both sides to allow them to continue making their illicit liquor. On Sunday, February 6, 1927, Jack Hall picked up a friend, Ernest Shelton, to go with him to help arrest David Cox. Most everyone gathered for a social afternoon at the John Chaney house. This house was located exactly where Fayerdale Hall, a conference center, now stands at Fairy Stone State Park in Patrick County, Virginia. Figuring that David Cox would be at the Chaney residence, Hall and Shelton headed there to make the arrest. And sure enough, Cox was there. However, he had become ill and was resting in a bedroom. When Hall and Shelton arrived at the Chaney house, they entered and found Cox asleep in a bed. They carefully removed a pistol from Cox's person and woke him to inform him that he was under arrest. In the meantime, the teenager, E.N., who started the whole feud, was also at the Chaney house. EN looked out the window and saw David Cox's brother, Maynard, coming up the road in his car. EN could not wait to run out and meet Maynard to tell him that Jack Hall and Ernest Shelton were at the house to arrest his brother David. Maynard ran up the hill and found Hall and Shelton holding their guns on David. Just as Maynard entered the room, Jack Hall shot David, killing him instantly. Maynard returned fire and killed Hall. Ernest Shelton reacted by shooting and killing Maynard Cox. Shelton reportedly continued wildly shooting and wounding at least two more people in the home. Shelton was arrested for the shootings. His father hired an attorney in Stuart, Virginia, to represent his son, paying the attorney almost $2,000. Shelton was acquitted of all wrongdoing. The murder of the Cox brothers created a lot of animosity between several families in the community. The Coxes were well thought of and respected. The smoke had settled, but the shooting was not over! One family, the Hollys, was particularly distraught over the murders. Five years passed, and then shooting again erupted on a November night in 1932. Henry Holly and his son Robert learned that Ernest Shelton would be sitting with the body of another man who had been murdered in an unrelated incident. It was customary, at that time, to sit with the body of someone who had died until time for burial. Under the cover of darkness, the Hollys crept to the Ike Prater house where Ernest Shelton was supposed to be sitting with the body. They hid outside the house, and after a while, they saw Shelton pass in front of a window. They opened fire, shooting multiple times through the window. After they stopped shooting, Henry and Robert Holly forced their way into the Prater house and found Shelton lying dead on the floor. Robert left the house, but his father stayed inside and began to argue with Ike Prater. Holly struck

Prater with a fatal blow over the head with his shotgun. Another person, Harold Quinn, who had also been in the home, noticed a pistol, lying on the floor, which had fallen from Shelton's person when he was shot. Fearing that Holly would leave no witnesses to his crimes, Quinn grabbed the pistol and killed Henry Holly. People still, to this day, discuss, argue about, and speculate about a teenager's thirst for illegal whiskey and the MOONSHINE MURDERS.

Fayerdale Hall, at Fairy Stone State Park, now stands where the old John Chaney House was located. The Chaney home was the site of three moonshine related murders on February 6. 1927.

Modifications, NASCAR, and Dirty Tricks

Cars became popular with the general public and became a necessary tool for the bootlegger. Cars were loaded to the max with cases of moonshine to be delivered to waiting customers. As time was money, the moonshiners didn't waste time while driving with their precious load. They typically knew only one speed, WIDE OPEN. Of course, their driving tactics often captured the attention of the Federal revenuers, state police, local police, and anybody else who wanted to chase them. Moonshiners spent many hours fine tuning their engines to get the maximum speed from their whiskey hauling machines. Of course, the moonshiners had to practice their high speed driving techniques to get a "feel" for their cars and how they handled on the narrow, curvy mountain roads. It was common practice for "good old boys" to get together on Sunday afternoons and race on the roads where they would later transport their illegal loads. This activity eventually spread to public races at small tracks or county fairs. The racing became so popular that sometimes thousands gathered and paid to watch. Drivers/moonshiners like Junior Johnson and Curtis Turner became folklore legends. A gentleman named Bill France recognized the potential for organized racing and set up a meeting with some of the drivers in 1948 at Daytona Beach. And the National Association of Stock Car Automobile Racing (NASCAR) was born. Today, organized racing is a multi-billion dollar business, and it all started from a few little stills in the backwoods of Appalachia! Not only did the moonshiners work on their cars to increase speed, but they also made modifications to utilize every inch of space to cram in as many cases of moonshine as possible. The back seat, and often the front passenger seat, would be removed. The wall between the back seat and the trunk would be removed to create one large opening behind the driver. These cars would be hidden most of the time unless they were being used in the moonshining endeavor. I worked at a "general store" when I was in high school in the early 60s. At that time, moonshining was very prevalent in our area. Restrictions had been placed on storekeepers, limiting the number of jars and the amount of sugar they could keep in inventory. But, entrepreneurial store owners overcame this problem by buying from multiple suppliers and maintaining the inventory stashed at a location away from the store. Computers were non-existent, and tracking the flow of moonshine ingredients was nearly impossible. I spent several hours loading sugar and jars into vehicles like the ones described above. Another vehicle modification frequently used by moonshiners involved the suspension system. A heavy load of sugar or a load of 'shine would cause the car's rear end to sag significantly. A law enforcement officer might notice this sag and suspect foul play was afoot. A new invention, the air shock, was ideal for the moonshiner. Several customers, who I loaded sugar for, had air shocks. They would stop by the store after loading, pump the shocks up to level the rear end and be on their way. Other gadgets were sometimes employed on the moonshiner's cars, which would impress old 007 himself. Some cars had a tank that would dump oil on the road with the push of a button or the pull of a lever. Another trick was similar. Instead of an oil slick, a container of roofing nails might be dumped. Another trick was releasing a concoction that created a dense smoke cloud you couldn't see through. Can you imagine being a revenuer chasing a moonshiner on a moonless night on a mountain road, not a great deal wider than your car? Your police light is reflecting off the trees, partially obscuring your vision. The wailing of your siren is breaking your concentration. You enter a hairpin turn. Your screaming tires are clawing for a grip on the narrow road, and suddenly your car hits an oil slick, all four tires burst, or the road totally disappears. This scenario usually ended in death for the officer as the moonshiner sped away in his "souped-up" machine. And the battle goes on.

Strong Medicine

Many people believed, and still do, that moonshine possesses strong medicinal capabilities. Moonshine rubbed on the gums of a young child, who was cutting teeth, was said to relieve the pain. A mixture of moonshine and sugar was reportedly a sure cure for a sore throat. I had a friend who claimed moonshine would cure his common cold. He would place his hat on the bedpost and crawl into bed. He would sip moonshine until he saw two hats and drift off to sleep. When he awoke, his cold would be gone. Another friend decided he would stop drinking. He told me that he only kept one pint of moonshine to cure snake bites. He then confessed that he almost froze to death during the winter, TRYING TO FIND A SNAKE!!!!

Franklin County
Sure Must Be a Sweet Place

During the Prohibition and Great Depression era, moonshine production exploded. One day, sales executives of a large, well known sugar company were reviewing sales records. They discovered Franklin County, Virginia, had purchased more sugar than New York City. Wondering how in the world a small mountain county in Virginia with a population of fewer than fourteen thousand people could use more sugar than a sprawling city of seven million, the company's vice president decided to come down and see for himself. As the story goes, the sugar executive traveled, by rail, to Ferrum. When the train pulled into the station, the VP was anxious to get out in the area and visit all the fabulous bakeries and candy factories buying all the sugar. Word has it that when he stepped from the train onto the platform, he took one look all around and stepped back on the train. While shaking his head, he exclaimed, "I know what's going on in this place!" and returned to New York.

Moonshiners and That Sinking Feeling

The last place you might expect to find a moonshine still could be on a hilltop on Deer Island in the middle of Philpott Lake, a US Army Corps of Engineers lake in Franklin, Patrick, and Henry Counties of Virginia. But that's precisely where two enterprising moonshiners chose to locate a large submarine still to take advantage of Philpott Lake's pure, crystal clear water. The still was over one hundred yards from the water, but the innovative bootleggers used an irrigation pump to pump water through a hidden pipeline from the lake to their still. The men used a small rowboat to bring in their supplies and to carry out their 'shine. Everything went smoothly for a while, but a "tragedy" was about to strike, as it does with most illegal activities. One night after a good run, the men were ready to bring out a load of their recently made moonshine. They carefully loaded the little rowboat with a large quantity of their whiskey and climbed in. They began a short paddle to the shoreline where their truck was parked. However, they had overloaded the boat, causing it to swamp and sink to the bottom of the lake, taking with it all the moonshine. Our entrepreneurs were a little soggy, but only their pride was hurt.

Months later, the combined effects of a drought and high demand for hydropower from Philpott Lake caused a significant drop in the water level. One of the moonshiners, while visiting the lake, noticed something between the main shoreline and Deer Island. IT WAS THE BOAT!!! With the help of an old JEEP, the determined moonshiners navigated through the mud and muck and reached the little boat. Much to their surprise, the moonshine was still in the boat, and the jars were tightly sealed and intact. They retrieved the moonshine and happily delivered it to their thirsty customers. That moonshine was probably "aged" more than any other 'shine in Franklin County!!!

Moonshiners used an irrigation pump to pump water to their still located near the top of Deer Island on busy Philpott Lake.

CHAPTER 7:
THE RAID

Revenuers used many investigative techniques to find illegal moonshining operations. In the early days, some industrious officers walked the hollows which contained a stream. The revenuers knew that a good supply of cold, clear mountain water was necessary for the moonshiner to make his illicit whiskey.   The revenuers routinely looked for tracks and other signs of human activity on old logging roads. They also frequently "touched base" with store owners who may have sold mash ingredients to a moonshiner. Revenuers would inquire about purchasers of corn meal, sugar, yeast, and jars.

In many cases, the store owner would protect his moonshining customers and not tell the authorities anything about his sales. However, he might provide information about everything he knew if he was threatened with being charged as an accomplice! Competition between moonshiners was very prevalent, especially during Prohibition (1922-1930), when all legal whiskey was banned. As discussed earlier, the moonshining industry exploded during Prohibition as many people seized the opportunity to fill the demand void for whiskey by supplying illegal moonshine. Some moonshiners would report a fellow moonshiner to eliminate the competition.

In some cases, the revenuers would make a deal with a small operator, who had been caught, to inform on or set up a larger operator or a major supplier of ingredients. It was the old principle of "using a small fish to catch a larger fish." In this type of case, the small operator would have his charges dismissed or reduced if he produced good information. Road checks were also routinely conducted in hopes of catching a moonshiner when he was making a delivery or bringing his illegal whiskey from the still site. Revenuers constantly conducted surveillance on known or suspected moonshiners to learn their patterns and habits. In more modern times, airplanes and helicopters were used to look in a likely wooded hollow.   Often, good tips were received from well-meaning citizens, which could also lead to the destruction of a still and the arrest of its owner. Most of the law enforcement techniques described above are still used today. When a moonshiner was caught and arrested at an operating still, he was usually charged with "Manufacturing Untaxed Whiskey." If someone was just caught with moonshine, they could be charged with "Possession of Untaxed Whiskey." People who furnished sugar, meal, yeast, and other supplies or provided other aid to the moonshiner could face a "Conspiracy to Manufacture Untaxed Whiskey" charge. All of these charges are serious and carry heavy fines and long periods of incarceration. In addition, it is important to remember that the mere possession, without a license, of any component of a still (kettle, cap, worm, etc.) is illegal under Virginia law. So if you are saving Uncle Joe's still as a family relic, you are committing a crime!!! When revenuers raided a still, they destroyed and/or seized everything. The still kettle, thumper, and flake stand were chopped up with an axe. Any barrels of mash would be poured on the ground and the barrels chopped up. Any buckets or tubs would also be chopped. Large operations or stills made from heavier gauge metal were sometimes destroyed with dynamite. The cap and worm were typically seized and presented as evidence when the case went to court. All moonshine would be poured out, and the jars would be broken. In more modern times, a small amount of moonshine would be saved for lab analysis. Legal whiskey has additives placed in it to enable laboratory technicians to distinguish it from illicit moonshine. The additives are referred to as congeners. The following accounts describe several local moonshine raids. Although these accounts are from Franklin, Floyd, and Patrick Counties in Southwest Virginia, raids like these occurred all over the Appalachian Mountains.

Moonshining charges are serious. Heavy fines, jail time, and loss of many personal rights are part of getting caught.

A revenuer empties a barrel of the mash during a raid.

When a revenuer destroyed something, he REALLY
destroyed it.

State Agents Destroy Moonshine Operation (1989)

State agents destroyed one of the largest moonshine operations in Patrick County's history. Agents found the illegal distillery secluded behind camouflage netting near Charity. The still could produce nearly 2,000 gallons of illicit whiskey per week. The operation was partly concealed in a mobile home and garage. A buried electrical line from the mobile home to the still allowed the moonshiners to pump whiskey through pipes to the garage, where it was bottled in one-gallon plastic jugs. ABC agents searched the home, but no one was arrested. The distillery consisted of sixteen 800 gallon stills and one 400 gallon still. Agents destroyed the distillery. Inside the home and barn, agents discovered over 2,000 pounds of wheat bran, Over 3000 plastic jugs, Mason jars, and fuel oil to cook the mash.

Franklin County Moonshine Stills Raided (1996)

ABC agents seized eight stills and 500 gallons of moonshine in a barn. Special Agent Beheler of the Virginia Department of Alcoholic Beverage Control Authority stated that agents raided a barn in the Truevine area of the county. He said they had been investigating the site before the raid. A truck was seized as well. Agents arrested a 23 year old Pittsylvania

County man and a 41 year old Franklin County man. Both men were charged with manufacturing untaxed whiskey. They were released on bond.

Penhook Man Arrested for Moonshining (2013)

A Penhook man is behind bars following a nine month moonshine investigation. According to the Virginia Department of Alcoholic Beverage Control Authority, special agents raided a still location in Franklin County. They found two 800 gallon operating stills. Agents also seized 1,600 gallons of mash and over 180 gallons of untaxed whiskey.

Patrick County Investigators and Virginia ABC Agents Raid Moonshine Still (2002)

While walking along a Patrick County creek looking for a possible marijuana patch, a Patrick County Investigator walked up on an 800 gallon submarine still. The still was being heated by a propane heater to preheat the mash to speed up the fermentation process. The Investigator carefully slipped away. Several days later, Patrick County officers and agents of the Virginia ABC destroyed the still. One person fled on foot but was soon arrested. Sugar, yeast, and Mason jars were seized and later destroyed.

Elamsville Man Arrested in Still Raid (2003)

A Patrick County man was arrested in a late night raid at his residence in the Elamsville section of Patrick County. Patrick County officers and agents of the Virginia ABC conducted the raid. A search warrant was executed at the residence following an investigation sparked by information provided by two different confidential informants. A basement still and 9 barrels of mash, in varying stages of fermentation, were destroyed at the residence. Several cases of moonshine were discovered and seized from a nearby junked car.

Two Moonshine Stills Destroyed in Vesta (2005)

A small pot still and a large submarine still were destroyed in a mountainous area of Patrick County. The pot still was set up and ready to run. A series of connected hoses from a nearby residence provided water for the still. Searching the surrounding woods revealed a newly constructed 800 gallon submarine still. Both stills were destroyed. A search warrant of the residence turned up a small quantity of methamphetamine and several pieces of drug paraphernalia. The male occupant of the dwelling was arrested for several drug and alcohol violations. The Virginia ABC and

Patrick County Sheriff's Office officers conducted the raid.

Operation Lightning Strike (1999 – 2001)

The joint Federal and state attack on illegal moonshine manufacturing in Virginia referred to as Operation Lightning Strike, was the most recent battle in the centuries old war between moonshiners and the Federal government. During the three year operation, authorities disrupted a multimillion dollar ring which supplied tons of sugar, bottling supplies, distilling equipment, and miscellaneous ingredients capable of making thousands of gallons of moonshine. Twenty six of the more than thirty people charged in the operation pled guilty to their charges, with some sentences reaching almost five years imprisonment. Officials stated one operation was shut down, which had been in business for over 30 years! Operation Lightning Strike also closed down a business in Rocky Mount. Officers stated the business sold enough sugar to manufacture over 1 million gallons of illegal moonshine.

Moonshine Case Tried in Floyd (1993)

An illegal moonshining operation resulted in the arrest of a Patrick County father and son. The still, located in Floyd County near the Blue Ridge Parkway, was raided and destroyed by Virginia state ABC agents. At the Floyd County Circuit Court trial, the father pled guilty to "Manufacturing Untaxed Whiskey." He was sentenced to one year in jail and given a $250 fine. All active jail time was suspended except 30 days. The 19 year old son was also found guilty. His case was taken under advisement.

Moonshine Operation Discovered in a Fake Cemetery (1979)

Probably one of the best plots EVER to hide a still occurred in the Henry Community of Franklin County, Virginia. The innovative moonshiners dug a large ditch that was big enough to hold eighteen 800 gallon submarine stills. The ditch was covered with a wooden roof that was painted green. Cement blocks were painted white and stacked, evenly spaced, to simulate tombstones. Artificial flowers were even placed on the "graves!" A stairway led to the fake cemetery, which was on top of a small knoll. A road leading to the cemetery was also disguised. Pipes were buried at the entrance. Pine trees were cut, and the trunks were inserted in the pipes to look like naturally growing trees. The moonshiners only had to pull the trees from the pipes to drive into the cemetery to unload supplies and pick up their illicit whiskey. From the highway and the air, the area looked like one of the many small family cemeteries common in the mountains of Virginia. When the still was raided by Federal and State agents, two men escaped on foot, and a third man was arrested. The stills and supporting equipment were destroyed with dynamite. In addition, the agents seized over 400 gallons of illegal moonshine and destroyed over 11,000 gallons of mash.

A Revenuer examines a "tombstone," which was located in a fake cemetery. The cemetery covered an underground room that contained a large moonshining operation.

Early revenuers pose with a seized moonshine still.

The following pictures are the remnants of old stills which have been raided. These stills are from the Patrick, Franklin, and Floyd County areas. The revenuers most often used axes to destroy illegal stills.

These twin submarine stills were probably raided in the 1950s. Note the axe marks.

Revenuers knew their axe cuts could be patched, especially on the submarine stills. To discourage the moonshiner from returning to the 'shine business, revenuers always seized the cap and worm. These components were more difficult to replace.

This Patrick County still is interesting in two ways. It is rare to see a still fabricated from 55 gallon steel drums. The steel is approximately 1/8 inch thick and is impossible to destroy with an axe.
Revenuers resorted to destroying this still with dynamite. Notice the holes in the still have been blown out from the inside of the drum.

This 800 gallon "sub" was operating near Philpott Lake in Franklin County.

This old submarine operation was raided near Shooting Creek in Franklin County. Shooting Creek was named for the early pioneers who settled in the surrounding mountains. They periodically gathered at the creek to have shooting matches with their muzzleloader rifles. Prizes included BEEF, PORK, and of course, MOONSHINE.

Old raided stills can be found on most any mountain hollow that contained a nice free flowing stream.

Looks like someone may have salvaged some parts
from this old kettle still. Wonder who's cookin'?

The submarine still became the most preferred type of still due to being easy and relatively inexpensive to fabricate.

CHAPTER 8:
JIMMIE RORRER – THE LEGEND

Jimmie Rorrer served as a Deputy Sheriff in Patrick County, Virginia, before becoming a Special Agent with the Virginia Alcohol Beverage Control Authority (ABC). Jimmie earned the respect of other law enforcement officers and lawbreakers as well. He aggressively performed his duties without bias or prejudice. Jimmie earned a reputation for his uncanny ability to discover and destroy illegal moonshining operations. Being a State officer, Rorrer worked in multiple areas of Virginia but did most of his work in Patrick and surrounding counties. Jimmie used some unusual but effective techniques to apprehend the mountain-smart moonshiners. Jimmie was known to put on a disguise and travel, on occasion, to far Southwest Virginia, where he would be locked up in jail with known moonshiners. He would befriend the moonshiners and eventually be invited to join them at their still site once everyone finished their jail time. You can guess the outcome of those encounters! Another example of Jimmie's observation skills occurred in the Charity area of Patrick County. Rorrer suspected a local resident was making moonshine. He had been sneaking onto the property before daylight to conduct surveillance in hopes of locating the still. During the time Jimmie had spent conducting surveillance, he had memorized every feature of the surrounding land. One morning, on return to his hiding place, Jimmie noticed something different. At the end of a field, Rorrer had seen a large brownish colored piece of pine brush. But on this morning, there was a large GREEN piece of pine brush. Upon examination, when the brush was pulled back, Jimmie discovered the hidden entrance to an underground room that contained, you guessed it, a nice copper moonshine still. During Jimmie's career in the 60s, 70s, and 80s, he took a lot of photographs of the still operations before they were destroyed. At this writing, Jimmie has been gone for 32 years. His son Darrell followed in his father's footsteps by becoming a Deputy Sheriff in Patrick County. Now retired, Darrell kept Jimmie's photographs and graciously shared them with me. In the previous chapter, you saw some old stills after being raided. Now, thanks to Darrell, you can see them while they were operating.

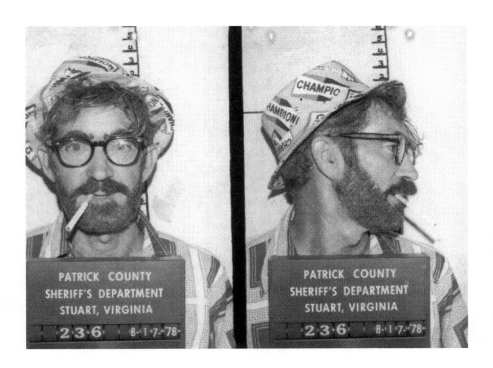

Meet Special Agent Jimmie Rorrer! Jimmie was known to put on a disguise and get locked up to gather intelligence on known moonshiners.

This is not your normal "outhouse." A set of steps
leads to an underground room containing a big old still.

Agent Rorrer (L) dismantles a still in an underground room. Note the stairway on the right.

A field full of moonshine!!!! These are one gallon plastic jugs filled with moonshine seized by Jimmie.

Remember the twin subs from the previous chapter?
This is the "before version." Then Jimmie busted
them!!!!

This large submarine operation could produce over 1000 gallons of moonshine per week.

It looks like the moonshiner was in the process of mashing-in, in this submarine still. Note the mash rake in the still.

That dynamite sure does make a mess!!

This truck was loaded and ready to make a delivery.
But Rorrer first delivered a new "visitor" to the Patrick
County Jail.

Another large operation that could produce over 1000 gallons of 'shine per week.

This still has some very elaborate plumbing!!!

A good view of the worm and flake stand.

A nice copper kettle still awaits the axe!!!

This still was cookin' and in full operation when it was raided.

Special Agent Jimmie Rorrer poses with this unique still made from 55 gallon steel drums.

CHAPTER 9:
CONCLUSION

Many books end with the words "THE END." However, we won't do that because it is very doubtful that moonshining is near the end. It has been going on for hundreds of years, with its beginnings rooted in the strong-willed Scotch-Irish immigrants. They were determined to make a living to support their families in a New World thousands of miles from their ancestral home. Moonshining has evolved from a small "pot" still located in some secluded backwoods hollow to large, organized operations capable of producing thousands of gallons of illegal whiskey per week. Demand is high. Moonshine is cheap.

The price may range from 10 to 25 percent of the "store-bought" stuff. This translates to about 50 cents a shot in some of the Northern nip joints. Many mountain traditionalists just prefer the harsh taste of that "good old mountain dew." Moonshine may have touched the people along the Appalachian Mountains more than anything. Tales about grandpa's still, the reference to moonshine in the country and bluegrass songs, movies, TV programs about moonshine, legendary car chases, and a NASCAR race on Sunday afternoon are all rooted in moonshine. No, we can't stop with something as final sounding as "THE END." So, let's just call this page a jumping off point for me and a starting point for the next author with a whole bunch of new stories about our backwoods chemists. And always remember, when you're outside on a dark, cloudy night, that, somewhere, THE "MOONSHINES" BRIGHT OVER THE VIRGINIA MOUNTAINS.

Index

A

B

C

cap, 21, 25, 37, 42, 43, 53, 61, 63, 131, 150

cemetery, 145, 147

Chaney, 107, 112

Charity, 136, 158

Chestnuts, 95

Christmas, 31

Civil War, 14

Commonwealth's Attorney, 32

Confederate, 14

copper, 41, 59, 60, 159, 173

Copper, 62

Copperhead Road, 78

Corn, 24, 78

corn squeezins, 74

Curtis Turner, 114

D

Daddy's Moonshine Still, 78

Darrell, 159

David Cox, 104

Deer Island, 122, 124, 125

DeHart, 96

distillery, 91, 94, 96, 136

Dupont,, 185

E

Elamsville, 140

EN, 103

English, 7

Ernest Shelton, 108

F

Fairy Stone, 76, 84, 87, 103, 112, 185

Fayerdale, 87, 95, 97, 107, 112

Federal, 9, 10, 14, 92, 106, 113, 142, 146, 185

Ferrum, 121

flake stand, 47, 49, 131, 172

flame-up, 73

Floyd, 87, 132, 143, 149

foreshots, 71, 79

Franklin, 29, 69, 78, 87, 120, 122, 124, 132, 137, 138, 144, 149, 152, 153

Franklin County, 29, 69, 78, 120, 124, 137, 138, 144, 152, 153

furnace, 41, 52, 63

G

Goblintown, 95

M

Martin, 2, 3, 185

mash, 23, 25, 26, 28, 31, 35, 37, 38, 39, 41, 42, 62, 63, 68, 88, 127, 131, 134, 137, 138, 139, 140, 146, 167

mashing-in, 25, 128

Mason jars, 137, 139

Maynard, 108

Maynard Cox, 108

methamphetami ne, 141

methyl, 58, 71

moonshine, 12, 14, 18, 19, 23, 27, 28, 31, 36, 41, 44, 46, 50, 54, 59, 65, 71, 75, 76, 78, 80, 83, 85, 87, 96, 98, 103, 112, 113, 116, 119, 120, 122, 124, 128, 130, 136, 137, 138, 140, 142, 146, 148, 158, 164, 166, 178, 185

mountain dew, 74, 178

Mountain Dew, 78

mule, 75, 89, 99, 100

N

NASCAR, 113, 115, 178

New York, 76, 120

nip joints, 76, 178

NO BUSINESS MOUNTAIN, 103

Norfolk and Western, 91, 93, 95, 97

O

Operation Lightning Strike, 142

P

Patrick, 59, 76, 83, 84, 85, 87, 103, 106, 122, 132, 136, 139, 140, 141, 143, 149, 151, 157, 169, 185

Penhook, 138

Pennsylvania, 10

Philpott, 91, 95, 97, 122, 124, 125, 152

pop-skull, 64

W

Washington, 10
whiskey, 7, 8, 9,
10, 11, 13, 15,
17, 18, 22, 29,
31, 46, 72, 75,
77, 91, 94, 95,
97, 98, 104,
113, 123, 127,
128, 129, 136,
138, 145, 177
**Whiskey
Rebellion**, 10
White Lightning,
74, 78
Woods, 102
worm, 47, 49, 56,
61, 63, 71, 79,
131, 150, 172

X

Xs, 46, 54

Danny Martin examines a broken piece of a crosscut saw found at an old raided still site.

About the Author

Danny Martin has had a very diverse working career. He received his degree in Mechanical Engineering from Virginia Tech in 1972. He furthered his education by earning his Master of Science Degree in 1976. Danny has been a math teacher, an engineer with Goodyear and Dupont, a Park Ranger with the Federal and Virginia State Governments, and an Investigator with the Patrick County, Virginia, Sheriff's Office. Coming from a sawmill family and with his work as a Park Ranger and his love for hunting, Martin has spent many hours in the woods. During his time in the woods, he has found the ruins of many old, raided moonshine stills. He also discovered and participated in the raids of active stills while working as an Investigator. Danny is currently an Interpretive Ranger with Fairy Stone State Park in Stuart, Virginia. As part of his job, he conducts a hike to the ruins of two stills while explaining the moonshining process along the way. He loves history and loves to share the knowledge he has gained about the impacts that moonshining had on the local mountain culture. He also hopes you like the book!!!!!